THE LAMP OF THE INTELLECT
OF SEVERUS IBN AL-MUQAFFA'
BISHOP OF AL-ASHMŪNAIN

CORPUS
SCRIPTORUM CHRISTIANORUM ORIENTALIUM

EDITUM CONSILIO

UNIVERSITATIS CATHOLICAE AMERICAE
ET UNIVERSITATIS CATHOLICAE LOVANIENSIS

Vol. 366

SCRIPTORES ARABICI

TOMUS 33

THE LAMP OF THE INTELLECT
OF SEVERUS IBN AL-MUQAFFA'
BISHOP OF AL-ASHMŪNAIN

TRANSLATED

BY

R.Y. EBIED AND M.J.L. YOUNG

LOUVAIN
SECRÉTARIAT DU CorpusSCO
WAVERSEBAAN, 49
1975

ISBN 2 8017 0016 9

Imprimerie Orientaliste, s.p.r.l., Louvain (Belgique)

D/1975/0602/8

INTRODUCTION

I. The Subject-matter of the Work

The Lamp of the Intellect begins with a foreword addressed to an unnamed Christian who had asked Ibn al-Muqaffaʿ to write a short exposition of the Christian faith for the instruction of the Coptic faithful. Accordingly, Ibn al-Muqaffaʿ presents his exposition under seventeen heads :

I. *The Creator* : after defining the Creator as Father, Son and Holy Spirit, Ibn al-Muqaffaʿ discusses the nature of the Deity in terms of the doctrines of Hellenistic philosophy. He also shows his acquaintanceship with the doctrines of Mani, Marcion, Bar Daisan and others. He only refers to Biblical passages to establish the equation of Spirit=Life.

II. *The Divine Hypostases* : under this heading the author touches upon Coptic monophysite doctrine, and offers no proofs from the Bible. With justification he refers to this as « the most subtle point in our doctrine », and rightly opines that whoever can understand this will be able to understand any theological doctrine.

III. *Christ* : the author provides explanations of this appellation and of the terms « Messiah » and « Son of God ».

IV. *The Incarnation* : this doctrine is explained as being the means whereby God has made known His reality through the immediacy of sight and hearing to His servants, just as He revealed Himself face to face to the prophets of the Old Testament, from which a number of verses are adduced.

V. *The Prophets and Apostles* : under this heading Ibn al-Muqaffaʿ gives a short statement of belief in the veracity of the prophets of the Old Testament, and denounces the Manichaean doctrine that Yahweh was to be equated with the evil principle.

VI. *Food, Drink, Crucifixion and Death of Christ* : this is the longest of the seventeen chapters. It contains an exposition of the true humanity of Jesus, together with some general discussion bearing on the relationship of the soul to the body. In this chapter the author makes much use of analogy to illustrate his doctrines. It would appear also that his quotations from the Bible were often made from memory, if we may judge from his erroneous mention of « the seed of David » in a quotation from the Epistle to the Hebrews.

VII. *The Resurrection* : this is a short statement of belief regarding the hereafter. The life of the blessed is described in non-material, abstract terms, but that of the damned in material terms of fire and worms.

VIII. *The Laws of Religion* : this somewhat misleading title is given to a short chapter dealing with God's omnipotence and man's freewill.

IX. *Prayer* : Under this rubric Ibn al-Muqaffaʿ deals briefly with the correct state of mind in which to offer prayers, the canonical hours of the church, and the supreme importance of the Lord's Prayer. He refers the reader to the work of Gregory of Nyssa for a more extended treatment of the subject.

X. *Fasting* : this concerns the rules for observing the forty fast-days of Lent, and an appeal to church tradition as the authority for them. Ibn al-Muqaffaʿ also mentions that Wednesday and Friday in every week of the year must be observed as fast days, as well as a number of other occasions in the calendar.

XI. *Rest days* : a short statement of the Christian holidays or holy days, including Sunday.

XII. *Almsgiving* : an assertion of the necessity for giving alms, both to needy believers and to unbelievers.

XIII. *Food* : an exposition of the foods forbidden to the Christian, together with an avowal of the liberty of the individual to follow the customs of his country in regard to eating, where there is no specific Biblical prohibition.

XIV. *Specific Penalties and Judgments* : according to Ibn al-Muqaffa''s remarks under this head, penal law is a matter for each town and country to decide for itself; by implication the church has nothing to say on the matter, beyond the excommunication of criminals.

XV. *Marriage* : in dealing with the rules of the Coptic Church concerning marriage the author also alludes to the marriage customs of other churches, the Nestorian, Syrian, Nubian, etc. It is notable however that he merely states these differences without condemning them, in contrast to his practice in dealing with other topics.

XVI. *Divorce* : under this head the author has little more to say than that the Coptic Church allows only one ground for divorce, viz. adultery.

XVII. *Slaves* : Ibn al-Muqaffaʻ accepts slavery as part of the order of things, as did Muḥammad, but like the prophet of Islam he enjoins kindly treatment of slaves upon their owners.

II. Method of Translating the Text

The translator of the present work has to face the normal difficulties associated with Middle Arabic texts (erratic grammar, non-classical nominal forms, etc.), as well as a number of difficulties not necessarily associated with all Middle Arabic writing.

The first of these latter difficulties is connected with the disregard shown in our text for the diacritical points used in Arabic for distinguishing consonants from each other : in some cases only the context can decide how a word is to be read. For example, pairs of words such as *ṭāhir* and *ẓāhir* are written in an identical way, leaving their pronunciation to be inferred from the sense required by the passage in which they occur.

Another problem is posed by a frequently obscure syntax, sometimes arising from an uncertain use of conjunctions. This characteristic often gives the impression that the writer was formulating his sentences in his mind prior to writing them down in a language other than Arabic — in fact Ibn al-Muqaffaʻ may well have been thinking in Coptic although writing in Arabic [1].

A further difficulty is presented by the numerous Biblical quotations which often seem to have been cited from memory, and which diverge in greater or less degree from the wording of the original. Such « approximate » quotations have been introduced in the notes by « Cf. » [2]

The attempt has been made here to keep as close as possible to the original in the translation, indicating all words and phrases the addition of which is required by the sense by means of brackets.

In two or three places in the text individual words occur which are

---

[1] For the disappearance of Coptic as a literary language, see G. Graf, *Geschichte der christlichen arabischen Literatur*, Vol. II [Studi e Testi, 133 (Vatican City, 1947)], pp. 294-295.

[2] For a discussion of Ibn al-Muqaffaʻ 's Biblical sources, see F. R. Farag, « The Technique of Research of a Tenth-century Christian Arab Writer : Severus ibn al-Muqaffa » in *Le Muséon*, vol. 86 (1973), pp. 54-56.

quite illegible, and attention has been drawn to these in the appropriate places.

III. Select Bibliography

Assfalg, J. « Severos ibn al-Muqaffaʻ » in *Lexikon für Theologie und Kirche*, vol. IX (1964), p. 703.

Bellet, P. « Severus ibn al-Mukaffaʻ » in *New Catholic Encyclopaedia*, vol. XIII (1967), p. 144.

Blau, J. *A Grammar of Christian Arabic, based mainly on South-Palestinian Texts from the First Millennium* [C.S.C.O., vols. 267, 276, 279 — Subsidia, Toms. 27, 28, 29]. Louvain (1966-67).

Chébli, P. *Réfutation de Saʻīd ibn Baṭrīq (Eutychius) (Le Livre des Conciles)* in *Patrologia Orientalis*, vol. III (1909), pp. 121-242.

Farag, F. R. « The Technique of Research of a Tenth-Century Christian Arab Writer : Severus Ibn al-Muqaffa » in *Le Muséon*, vol. LXXXVI (1973), pp. 37-66.

Graf, G. *Geschichte der christlichen arabischen Literatur*, 5 Bde. [Studi e Testi 118, 133, 146, 147, 172 (Vatican City, 1944-53)].

—, « Zwei dogmatische Florilegien der Kopten » in *Orientalia Christiana Periodica*, vol. III (1937), pp. 49-77.

Jirjis, Murqus *Al-Durr al-Thamīn fī Īḍāḥ al-Dīn* (Cairo, 1925, reprinted 1971).

Labib, S. Y. « Ibn al-Muḳaffaʻ » in *The Encyclopaedia of Islam* (second edition), vol. III (1968), pp. 885-886.

Leroy, L. *Sévère ibn al-Moqaffaʻ évèque d'Aschmounain. Histoire des Conciles (Second Livre)* in *Patrologia Orientalis*, vol. VI (1910), pp. 465 ff.

Maiberger, P. « *Das Buch der Kostbaren Perle* » *von Severus Ibn Al-Muqaffaʻ* [Veröffentlichungen der Orientalischen Kommission, Bd. XXVIII (Wiesbaden, 1972)].

Troupeau, G. *Catalogue des Manuscrits Arabes*, Ière partie : Manuscrits Chrétiens, tom. I, Nos 1-323 (Paris, 1972).

THE LAMP OF THE INTELLECT

* In the name of the Father, the Son and the Holy Ghost, one God, we begin with the help of God most high and His gracious help, in writing *The Book of the Lamp of the Intellect* (or *The Book of Insight*), 5 concerning the whole range of Christian doctrines, composed by Father Anbā Severus, Bishop of al-Ashmunain, who was known before his entering religion as Abū al-Bishr ibn al-Muqaffaʿ the Scribe, may God grant us the blessing of his prayer. Amen.

In the name of the Father, Lord of All, Creator of the Heavens 10 and Earth, and of the Word appertaining to Sonship from eternity to eternity from Mary the Pure Virgin, Chosen and Preferred [above others], a corporeal person, a veil and a temple, and [in the name of] the Holy Spirit, One God.

May God preserve you from error and rescue you from your fool- 15 ishness and give you success [in achieving] sound speech and action.

You have mentioned the defamation of our doctrines by the opponents of our religion and [their] rejection of our statements [of belief], and that you have not found any book [1] by previous [authors] containing a description of the doctrines of the Christians in the form of an expo- 20 sitory summary, [able to] remove their doubts and explain the things which are difficult for them.

All our fellows whom you have encountered hold many untenable views in that which they enunciate and profess.

You have asked me that I should expound for you a summary of 25 our teachings, and make clear to you the ideas of our religion, since this is the most worthwhile and important part of what we have to explain and expound, because through it the ignorant person may be made mindful, and the learned person may be enlightened.

I find you have charged me with a momentous subject and assigned 30 me an important task, since the doctrine of the Christians [contains] subtle ideas and [requires] profound exposition. Only a wise, proficient, philosophical, learned, good person can understand it, as the books of God, blessed be His name, say in this regard.

The Prophet Hosea bears witness to this when he says : « Who is

---

[1] I.e. in Arabic.

wise ? The one who knows these things, and the philosopher, who perceives their meanings. » [2]

* p. 2   *Solomon also says : « Tell me what his name is and what his father's (sic) name is [3], if you know it »; he means the Creator.

The Gospel says : « No one knows the Son except the Father, and [no one knows] the Father except the Son » [4]. And he said : « I acknowledge Thee oh Father, since Thou hast hidden these things from the wise and clever and hast made them known to babes » [5]. Thus is Thy will and desire. He means by this the wise priests and clergy of whom God has said that « they are wise in flesh and not in knowledge », and he has also said that « they are blind of heart and eyes and deaf of ears to hear and see » [6]; and he means by « babes » the apostles, the clergy, the righteous fathers and the pure noble ones of whom [the Bible] says : « Blessed are the pure in heart, for they shall see God » [7], that is, they shall know Him, and He shall illumine their hearts with His knowledge, as David says : « I have seen the Lord on my right hand, and thus I shall not be moved » [8].

Therefore there is no need for me to [elaborate] what the books of God have proclaimed and explained; I do not have [enough] confidence in myself to make myself the equal of those whom I have mentioned, nor to compare myself with some [of those persons] I have described. I only seek a reward for my words about that Noble and Gracious Substance which is ineffable, and which is beyond any description. It is exalted above the similitude of creatures and the descriptions of created beings and those in authority over us.

May God give you help in relying upon obedience to our Creator and striving for what is wholesome for our life to come which we will obtain with our Lord, because life is short, and time is of little duration and death is near, and the punishment for laying down [erroneous] rules is great; but I did not wish to reject your request or refuse to fulfil your desire, and I have therefore followed the words

---

[2] Cf. *Ho.* 14, *9.*
[3] *Pr.* 30, *4.*
[4] *Mt.* 11, 27; *Jo.* 10, *14-17, 25, 26.*
[5] *Mt.* 11, *25.*
[6] Cf. *Is.* 42, *18.*
[7] *Mt.* 5, *8.*
[8] *Ps.* 16, *8.*

of the Gospel, which says : « If one asks thee, give to him; and whoever
seeks of thee, * do not refuse him » [9].   * p. 3

I have also followed the words of the apostle who says : « Help
and support ye whomsoever is weak in faith » [10].

5 I have entreated God, blessed and exalted be His name, and I
have told you what has been made known to me; I have informed
you of that in which I have been successful in [attempting] to understand and know. If it is right, it is from the Holy Spirit speaking
through our mouths, and uttering by means of our tongues; and if
10 it is wrong it is our shortcoming, weakness, error and heedlessness.

So do not take offence at our error, and may our fault not be gross
in your eyes. Be content with what we have set forth for you, for
we have laboured, explained, condensed and expounded, and have
refrained from arguing each point and refuting [our] opponents, for
15 these things are mentioned in the books which are suitable for them;
and from God comes success and support.

I. OUR STATEMENT REGARDING THE CREATOR,
BLESSED BE HIS NAME : FAITH IN THE ONE GOD

We know Him as Father, Son and Holy Spirit, one Substance
20 and one Nature and one Essence. We have said that He is Father,
Son and Holy Spirit, as the Gospel has instructed us. We have said
that He is one single substance : [this] means that His essence and
nature resemble nothing among created beings, nor correspond to
any essence among created beings, for His substance and essence
25 are unlike other simple [and] compound substances ...... [11]. We
refer to Him as being substance (for there is nothing but substance,
corporeality or accident, according to the statement of Julian, while
according to the logical philosophers existing things must be substance
or accident, and the body in their opinion is included in substance)
30 because proofs exist that He cannot * be body; otherwise He would be   * p. 4
subject to composition, division, dissolution, being, decay, time and
place; all these are qualities of created beings, and it is certain that they

---

[9] *Mt. 5, 42.*
[10] Cf. *Ro. 14, 1.*
[11] Text corrupt; eight unintelligible words are inserted here, the last four of which
are repeated at the top of the next folio.

are corporeal. Accident requires a vehicle to convey it and an attribute
by which it may be qualified. It is not truly existent, as the logicians
have shown, because so long as substance and body are not existent,
accident is not existent, and because accidents have no affects, no
permanence and no being except through other things.   5

There is agreement that the Creator, Who is great and glorious,
has not ceased to be existent, nor does He cease to exist, and that He
is active, not requiring, in His existence, any other person, because
He exists through His essence.

We have said that He is substance, since it is not possible for Him 10
to be a body or an accident. We do not hold the belief that He is the
substance which Aristotle has described in his Book of Logic, and
who claims that He reconciles opposites within His essence, because
he has described [in that book] the substance which is Socrates and
Plato. This substance is a primary, partial substance; we do not hold 15
that it is the secondary substance, i.e. the species and genus, because
these are merely images of the primary substance and take different
forms, depending upon whether they have [an independent principle
of] being in their essence, or are merely notional; we believe only that
He is existent through His essence, and is imperishable and everlasting, 20
because He is not like the accidents, which did not exist, and then
came into existence, nor like bodies, which although substances, yet
are composed of form and matter. We intend to convey that He is
different from all bodies, accidents and notional substances.

For He is truly existent, and has no need of anything else in His 25
existence : this is what we mean by saying « substance ». We only
use the term « one substance » because the pagans and idol-worshippers
and [the followers of] Mani, Bar Daisan and Marcion allege that the
Creator is various substances; and similarly Arius, Eunomios and
* p. 5 Plato the philosopher, * for the latter posits a number of creators.   30

We have refuted the views of all these with our statement that the
Creator of the world is one substance and not many substances.
Similarly with the doctrine of Aristotle that the Creator is the totality
of the world and that the universe is eternal, for we say that His
substance is one substance which does not resemble any of the world's 35
substances.

The meaning of our statement that He is Father, Son and Holy
Spirit : having received Divine Guidance from Him, we hold the belief
that this Creator lives and speaks, for His speaking is His Word, and

His life is His Spirit. His speaking is merely called « Son » in order to convey the meaning that it is born from His essence, because philologists call anything which is generated from the thing itself « son ». In this way they refer to Plato as the son of Ariston; that is, he
5 was of his essence, his substance and his nature, and he had no other physical origin. In some languages one talks of the crescent moon as having been « born », and of a palm, or [other] trees, as having been « born ».

These names, i.e. Father, Son and Holy Spirit, are among ones
10 employed by the ancients, which they attested and acknowledged. I refer to the ancient philosophers, including Hermes, Plato, Pythagoras, Eumenius and their like; it has been handed down in the ancient books. I make reference to their statements in *Kitāb al-Tawḥīd* [12].

15 Since we have explained the significance of our conception in calling God's Word « Son », [the need for] insistence and ingenuity [on this question] disappears, because our aim must be to attain correct concepts, rather than mere verbal designations. [This is] because names only exist by [mutual] agreement. This point has been
20 overlooked by our fellows in respect of calling the Word « Son » and the life « Spirit ».

As regards « life » being called « Spirit », this is clear, both from the Bible, as it says in the Psalms : « When thou takest away their breath, they fail » [13], that is « do away with their life », and from the phraseo-
25 logy of the philologists « I will annihilate your spirit », * that is, « destroy life and kill you », and from the words of the Torah : « The spirit of life which God put into Adam » [14]. The physicians assert that this is in the heart; and they also call life « perishable blood », for they point out that it is in the heart.

*p. 6

30 We say « Holy Spirit » because spirits are numerous, and we call devils spirits and angels spirits [also]. The phrase « Holy Spirit » is used because the devils are spirits which are not sanctified and are not clean. The angels also, although they are spirits, are subject to transitoriness, as has been described in the story of Satan : after being

---

[12] See GRAF, Zwei dogmatische Florilegien der Kopten, pp. 61-62.
[13] Cf. *Ps.* 104, *29*.
[14] Cf. *Gn.* 2, *7*.

obedient he turned to disobedience and was cast out, unclean and excluded.

Thus this Spirit was singled out with the designation « Holy », that it might be clear that it is something in which uncleanliness, filth and vice have no part.   5

This is the purport of our discussion concerning the Creator, Whose name is glorious, regarding the fact that He is essence, and that He is Father, Son and Holy Spirit, by way [of expressing this] in summary form.

II. OUR STATEMENT REGARDING THE DIVINE HYPOSTASES   10

What we mean by « Hypostases » is that since the nature of this essence is eternal and unchangeable, and has [infinite] duration, and is not like the qualities which exist and then come to an end, nor like the accidents which perish and deteriorate, the speech of the Creator, Who is blessed and exalted, is eternal and unchangeable, not like 15 the ephemeral evanescent speech of human beings, the sole cause of which is the mixture of the voice with the air, for eventually its syllables cease and come to an end. In contrast, His speech (He is blessed and exalted) is of His essence and of His substance, and does * p. 7 not need air * for it to be manifested, nor a voice for it to exist ; rather 20 its cause is contained in the essence [of God Himself], and it is therefore of His essence and of His existence, being self-existent, rational and intelligible, and is recognized by the intellect which knows that it is the speech of the essence of which it had had previous cognizance, and which has been proved to exist. The intellect distinguishes it 25 and gives it precedence ; it cannot conceivably be denied or rejected. For whoever denies the immutability and eternity of these attributes will have denied what he [himself] has acknowledged and will have denied something whose existence he has confessed, like the Jews and the Mu'tazilites, who make the attributes of the Creator's names 30 devoid of meaning.

Because we have said that we have presented it [15] here for the sake of concision and brevity, we think it appropriate to leave out the adducing of proofs and the refutation of opponents, because we have already done this in our book [written] against them [16].   35

[15] I.e. the foregoing discussion.

[16] Probably a reference to his work *Al-Bāhir fī al-Radd 'alà al-Yahūd wa 'l-Mu'tazilah*, which is listed in P. SBATH's *al-Fihrist*, No. 121, p. 21.

This is what we mean by « hypostasis ». We wish to convey that the attribute of this substance is eternal, immutable and rational, and is not perishable like accidents, nor is evanescent like voices and all human speech, and similarly with their life and spirits.

5 If someone expresses it by using the words « persons » or « characteristics » or « ideas » or « attributes », as the ancients did, and they mean by this its everlastingness, the meaning of their expressions is the same, although the terminology is different. Therefore understand and grasp this, for it is the most subtle point in our doctrine, 10 and whoever is conversant with it will find theological discussion straightforward and clear for him, and he will quickly grasp its significance, for we have brought it within range [of the understanding] and have expounded it in a way that not many of our fellows have previously done. I have also explained it in my book *Tafsīr al-* 15 *Amānah* [17].

III. Our Statement on Christ

Christ in our belief is the Word of God and His wisdom and His power, as the Bible says [18]. We call him * Christ following the word of * p. 8 God in His scriptures. Our fellows have been of different opinions 20 regarding calling the Word of God « Christ ». We shall explain this when we describe the ways in which the sects differ and the points on which they agree. This appellation was translated into the Greek language by the expression « the Anointed One ». Because he also referred to himself as « Christ » when the Samaritan woman addressed 25 him, we [also] accord him that [name], and because it is agreed that he is the Messiah, coming after the apostles and prophets.

The doctrine I hold in calling him the Word of God, he being singled out as Messiah, is the doctrine of some of the Fathers, to the effect that the Word was united with the flesh, and this union is the anointing, 30 for he was anointed because he had become incarnate; and « incarnation » is the way in which his « being anointed » is expressed. Just as that which provides his body with anointing is the oil, and oil is corporeal, so the Word of God is called « Messiah » because it has the attribute of being incarnated, just as the Son of God, when he was

---

[17] The full title of this work as given by Abū 'l-Barakāt ibn Kabar (GRAF, Zwei Dogmatische Florilegien der Kopten, p. 62) is *Tafsīr al-Amānah al-Urthuduksiyyah*.
[18] *1 Co.* 1, *24.*

born a second time, was named « Son »; yet he had been designated « Son » before that.

I say this in refutation of those of our fellows who oppose us, and who only accord the name of « Christ » to Christ at the time of the union, for [they claim] that this appellation may only be used of the 5 Messiah when the Word has united with the man.

I have explained everything relevant to this school of thought in my books [written] against them.

IV. Our Statement on the Incarnation

We say that the blessed God, as we have previously stated, is 10 possessed of refulgent power and penetrating will, and reveals Himself to His servants and shows Himself to His prophets and apostles, in order that they may be able to see Him, as the Bible describes. It tells us that He addressed Moses and Jacob, Jacob saying : « I saw the Lord face to face and yet my life is preserved » [19], and that He 15 revealed Himself to Abraham.

* p. 9   *Job said : « I had heard of thee by the hearing of the ear, but now we have seen thee with the eye » [20]. Isaiah said that he saw Him sitting on the throne with the cherubim and seraphim around Him [21]. Similarly with Daniel and Amos and Ezekiel.   20

The people of the Kingdom are unanimous that He is on the throne and that He is the One Sitting (Who is exalted) on the throne (He is exalted and glorious).

We hold His words to be true, believe His prophets and acknowledge what His books have stated, and we do not deny or reject... [22]. 25

We believe that the prophets saw Him (He is blessed and exalted) as I have described, in such a way that it would be possible for Him to be seen, but not for His essence to be perceived, nor for the sight to fall upon His essence, nor for it to see His substance. Our fellows have provided the most elegant commentary and most penetrating 30 interpretation of what the prophets have described in the way of visions and sitting on the throne. We have expounded it in the appropriate place; for He appeared to us and showed [Himself] in the fullness

---

[19] *Gn. 32, 30.*
[20] Cf. *Jb. 42, 5.*
[21] Cf. *Is. 6, 1-2.*
[22] The word *tawqīfan* appears to give no satisfactory sense.

of time in a body, which He had created from the body of the Virgin
Mary, and He caused us to hear His speech from the body with which
He had been united; He caused us to hear His words, as He caused
Moses to hear His speech and words from the [burning] bush and
5 the *shechinah*.

He also manifested Himself to the children of Israel, and addressed
them on the mountain, and caused them to hear His words.

Thus He has enabled us to participate in hearing His words and
speech, addressing us from His earth just as He addressed those
10 others from His heaven, and has commanded us, just as He commands His angels, from near at hand, and has drawn us near to Him,
just as the cherubim and seraphim, who are amongst His creatures,
have drawn near to Him. He has already (His name is blessed) notified
us that He deals with us in this way, for one of the prophets has said
15 that God shall in truth appear upon the earth and walk among men.
And another prophet has said : « He has lowered the heavens and
descended from them » [23]; [they] are His own creation; and He has
addressed mankind from them, as He did [from the burning] bush.
He has spoken to * His apostles from them, and from the earth which   * p. 10
20 He created; and He has spoken to [His] servants from them. The
body is His creation, and He has addressed His creatures from it.

This is our statement regarding His incarnation.

The question of His incarnation, and how something eternal could
be incarnated in something created, I have explained clearly, and I
25 have also made it clear in my book *Īḍāḥ al-Ittiḥād* [24]. I have analyzed
every pronouncement of every objector from the adherents of other
doctrines, and have discerned their corrupt nature, and so if you
wish [to inquire regarding them] consult [my remarks] there.

The One Who speaks to us from the body and Who is visible and
30 apparent, is the [same] One Who spoke to Moses from the clouds and
to Isaiah, Jeremiah and the rest of the prophets, and Who revealed
Himself to the chosen ones, Abraham, Isaac and Noah. That is what
we believe.

---

[23] Cf. *Ps.* 144, 5.
[24] Presumably identical with Ibn al-Muqaffaʻ's work *Fī 'l-Ittiḥād*, which is as yet
unpublished.

V. Our Statement on the Prophets and Apostles

We acknowledge and believe in all the prophets whom the Bible has described of old, and we acknowledge that all that they have announced is from God, Who is blessed and exalted, and that they are His messengers to His creatures and servants, and that all the 5 laws of the Torah, and that which it contains, is that for which all creatures serve God, century after century, and generation after generation, so that all of it is pure and beautiful and is devoid of anything which we would wish to deny or reject.

And [we believe] that the One Who spoke to Moses and the prophets 10 was the Creator, the Wise, the Generous, the Merciful, the Exalted; it is not so, as the accursed Mani says, that the lawgiver of the laws of the Torah and the one who spoke to Moses and the prophets of the Israelites was the Devil (our Lord is far exalted above his impiousness).

Rather, we acknowledge and confess and believe that all that the 15 prophets of the Israelites announced was the truth from God, and anything else is nugatory and false and void and slanderous, and that the Torah and the other books which our teachers composed are God's books and speech and laws and statutes and obligations and judgments. People continued to show them reverence until the coming 20 of Christ, who renewed the laws and repealed what * people in the past had approved, as an act of grace on his part, and he defined or appealed to the ideas of matters of good report, and announced religious obligations and laws of conduct in harmony with what the philosophers and wise men have laid down, and thus refuted the 25 slanderous statements of the accursed Mani, Marcion, al-Labān, Bar Daisan and others.

* p. 11

VI. Our Statement on the Food, Drink, Fatigue, Crucifixion and Death of Christ

When he became incarnate his incarnation was an incarnation of 30 a soul and an intellect totally and completely, that is he took upon himself complete manhood without any change of essence, and made it a temple and a place and a screen for himself, entering into a composite unity with it, as I have explained in my book on *Īḍāḥ al-Ittiḥād*. Since the case is as we have described it we have attributed 35 to him everything that we attribute to [other] bodies in regard to natural states.

By my words « natural states » I mean eating, drinking, tiredness and suffering, because every body requires food and drink to replace
5 that which has been digested ; a body is not able to forego this or be deficient in it, nor is an embodied person [like Christ], because he adopted this as [his] method and the inevitable dissolution and exposure to external influences which this involved. The proof of this is the saying of the apostle : « He did not take his form from the
10 angels, but from the seed of David » (sic) [25], and Basil has alluded to this same idea in one of his books.

No person can deny that the body takes nourishment to itself, experiences fatigue and is subject to external influences, as long as it is a body, resembling all other bodies, in the world of generation
15 and decay, because we affirm that * bodies after their resurrection   * p. 12 from their graves will not be in need of [anything], will not be under compulsion, and will not be subject to external influences, because they [will] have been formed with an unchanging structure that does not alter, as the apostle says : « This transient being shall put on
20 garments that shall not change, and this mortal shall not die » [26].

Bodies after resurrection will not be subject to any external influence, nor will they require food or drink, nor will they fall sick, nor will they grow old, nor decay nor change.

This applies to our doctrine, regarding the body of Christ after
25 his resurrection, that he did not need food or drink. As regards the words of the Gospel [27] about the fish and the honeycomb, he explained and made clear the reason for this.

Regarding the crucifixion and death [of Christ] we have said that the body which was taken was subject to everything to which other
30 mutable bodies are subject in the world of generation and decay ; the simple eternal essence was not affected in itself by any external influence, nor by suffering, because it is not something which is characterized by liability to suffering or mutability, and is not affected by decay ; and since it is simple, not compound, it is not possible
35 for it to be affected by sufferings, nor is it [in any way] deficient, since its nature and essence are not palpable or tangible.

[25] Cf. *Hb.* 2, *16.*
[26] *1 Co.* 15, *53.*
[27] *Lu.* 24, *42.*

External influences can only affect what is palpable or tangible, such as compound bodies and things like them. Our opponents are completely in error, because they suppose that we ascribe to the creative eternal essence what we ascribe to mutable, corruptible bodies. This supposition is erroneous; it cannot be maintained and is 5 not correct.

Christ from the point of view of his humanity and his incarnation was susceptible to pain, accidents, external influences and death; but from the point of view of his eternity and divinity was not palpable nor tangible, nor susceptible to suffering or death, as is the case with 10 a body that is united with being, or a soul that is united with a body, or a fire that is united with firewood; for the body is disposed to death, corruption, * mutability, subjection to the effect of dissolution and deliquescence, and localization in a [particular] place; but being is not characterized by any of these things, and similarly the soul 15 is not characterized by being mortal — it does not die, nor does it hunger or suffer thirst, even though it is united with a corruptible body which is mortal, which does suffer hunger and thirst. It is like fire, which, even when the firewood has turned to ash and has decayed, is not characterized by death and decay. There are numerous ana- 20 logies of this kind.

So whoever slanders us by saying that we maintain that God was killed and crucified and died, is ignorant of our statements, and una- ware of what we mean. If the common people were careful in expressing themselves errors would not occur on the part of the hearer; however 25 metaphorical usage in regard to nouns and figurative speech mislead many people. The Bible has described and explained this. I refer to what the Jews did to Christ, for it was a matter with which you are acquainted from the books of the ancients; if this were not so we would have explained it and commented upon it.   30

[Like other] people, you may say « the herb has sprouted, the palm-tree has grown tall, the tree has borne fruit, » when in fact the herb has not sprouted, the palm-tree has not grown tall and the tree has not borne fruit, for it is God (Who is exalted) Who has made 35 the herb sprout, Who has made the palm-tree grow tall and has made the tree bear fruit. For indeed the figurative usages in speech are many : for example people's saying « The sword has killed him », meaning by this « God has killed him and put him to death», and similarly with the person who says « He ate and drank and died », 40

* p. 13

when he means that it is the body, united with him, which really ate, drank and was killed.

That body is the body of Christ, and [such] characteristics apply to that which is incarnated in a body. For example, we say « Socrates
5 has fallen sick », meaning that his body has undergone change as a result of its natural functions; but Socrates' *soul* has not fallen sick, nor does it ever change in respect of the characteristics which apply to * the incarnated essence.   * p. 14

Similarly the [idea of] attribution applies to everything compounded
10 or conjoined or combined of various things, for it is characterized in every one of the essences in which are conjoined or compounded or combined all the essences. For example, when we say « Plato knew and understood » we mean that his soul knew and that his soul was the thing that « knew », because the body, *qua* body, does not know,
15 so that it cannot understand, but is indeed a mere clod [28], like stone, wood, iron or other bodies. And similarly when we say « Plato has eaten », we merely mean that his body has received food in compensation for what it has used up [29], for the soul does not eat, and is not characterized by alimentation. However the attributes are applied
20 to « Plato » as a whole, by way of clarification and exposition [in speech]. Similarly we say that Christ is a Creator and a Sustainer and Living, *qua* God; and we say that Christ has eaten and drunk and been killed and has died *qua* man. The two descriptions both apply to Christ, just as they apply to Plato and Socrates.

25   VII. Our Statement on the Resurrection

We believe in the revivification, general resurrection and the rising again of corruptible bodies on the Day of Resurrection, just as [we believe] that Our Father created Adam as the first man, and that [these bodies] will be in that [original] state and in that form,
30 whatever that might have been, and that the righteous who have obeyed the Creator and have acted according to His laws and ordinances will enter the Kingdom. When we say « Kingdom » we mean an everlasting, eternal state of being, whose people will have been freed from all needs and necessities and trials and constraint; they
35 will live a life of felicity, like that of * the angels. They will take pleasure   * p. 15

[28] Lit. « a stone like the stones ».
[29] Lit. « dissolved ».

in giving praises and glorifying [God]; they will not lust, nor will they suffer illness nor decrepitude nor pain, and they will not be under the constraint of the natural functions, that is, the [necessity for] food and drink and sleep and rest; rather they will have put on the garments of eternity and everlastingness, and will have been 5 furnished with uninterrupted, joyful life.

As the apostle says [30], the Kingdom of God is not food or drink. The Gospel says that there is no marriage or divorce there [31]. Plato said something similar to this about the gods, whom, he alleged, the Creator created, and to whom He entrusted the matter of the creation, 10 [although] they are mortal by nature; but He has safeguarded their essences from mutability and corruptibility.

Aristotle said : « The firmament is preserved by the power of the Creator from mutability and change and decay ».

As for those who disobey the prophets and apostles of God and 15 do not acknowledge His ordinances and laws, and disobey His command, they shall be punished by the fire of Hell and the outer darkness, and the worms which do not sleep, and other sorts of punishment of which God knows. As the apostle says : « Every man shall be requited for the actions his body has done; if they were good, with 20 good; if they were evil, with evil » [32].

All that we have mentioned regarding the felicity of the righteous and the punishment of the wicked is everlasting, without end or termination.

VIII. Our Statement Regarding the Laws of Religion   25

The laws of religion come after belief in God, Who is exalted, the One, the Substance, Creator of the World by His Word and all its powers by [means of] a Spirit in Him, and the acknowledgement that He possesses a Word and a Spirit, and that * His Speech and His Spirit shall never pass away, and shall not perish or decay like the 30 speech and spirit of created beings.

* p. 16

Rather, His Speech and His Spirit are from His essence and substance, while our speech and spirit are created, giving rise to our essences.

---

[30] *Ro. 14, 17.*
[31] Cf. *Mt. 22, 30.*
[32] Cf. *Ro. 2, 6.*

Then we have acknowledged the prophets and apostles as we have [previously] said, and [we have acknowledged] that the Creator, blessed is He, is just, generous, clement, knowing and powerful, and that nothing can frustrate Him, and that He is the Creator, the Knower,
5 the Founder of the World, the Founder of the Creation, both the visible and the invisible portions of it.

The primeval matter from which, the philosophers assert, [God] formed the world, is created, intelligible and caused, and the creation is not attributable to an angel, as the Jews say, nor to an inferior
10 deity, as Benjamin of Nihavend asserted, nor to the planets, as Plato says.

He created us capable and in control of our faculties, so that whatever things He commands us to do, which we [in fact] do, are in obedience to Him, and whatever things He forbids us to do, which
15 we [nevertheless] commit, are in disobedience to Him. All these things are our actions and deeds, [made possible] by the ability which we have been given to attain to His obedience and love, and to behave in accordance with His pleasure and will.

IX. Our Statement on Prayer

20 We have been taught that the prayers which we were commanded [to offer] by the apostles of Christ are [to be offered] seven times every day and night; if we wish we may combine these, or if we wish we may keep them separate, because He has made things easy for us and not strict in regard to their times.

25 The measure of prayer is turning towards Him, standing in His presence, acknowledging His lordship and deity, and glorifying His name and hallowing it.

We should prostrate ourselves in His presence, and should be humble and submissive to any extent we wish, for He has not laid
30 down any defined limit.

We consider that [our desire for] perfection [must be] the reason for our not carrying out anything other than the aforementioned duty.

Some of the Jews and a group of Muslims have asserted that who-
35 ever exceeds this is an ignorant heretic. Rather, [God] * has given us * p. 17
free choice in all of this, beyond the [fixed] conditions which we have already mentioned.

Whatever the individual does after formulating a sincere intention [to pray] and direct his mind, [he must] turn towards Him and raise his hands, and [show] fear and dread without thought or anger, as the apostle says : « I should like those at prayer to raise their hands in purity without thought or anger » [33]. Whoever does that will be 5 rewarded for it according to its great or little extent.

The times which have been fixed and in regard to which latitude is allowed, and which have been alluded to by the apostles, are the dawn prayer, [the prayer] when three hours of the day have elapsed, [the prayer] at the sixth hour of the day, [the prayer] at the ninth 10 hour, and also the evening prayer, which is before the setting of the sun, the prayer [just before] sleep and the midnight prayer [34].

We should recite during the prayer, beyond what Christ has taught us in his Holy Gospel [35], whatever Psalms and hymns we find suitable, and whoever knows nothing but that prayer [35] is to be regarded as 15 having done enough, because it combines everything that concerns faith, affirmation, glorification, praise, supplication, entreaty and petition.

Whoever wishes to appreciate this in regard to the exposition of the Gospel, let him consult [our work] [36], for we have there made clear 20 the significance of this prayer, with a commentary. Gregory, Bishop of Nyssa, has expounded it before our time in a more extended and elaborate way, in five discourses in which he elucidates this prayer, and has shown the benefit and great significance of prayer.

X. Our Statement on Fasting   25

As regards fasting, we are obliged to fast for forty days, these being unsullied by sin or wrongdoing, and He has commanded us to eschew depravity, immorality and fraudulence, and to avoid during [that * p. 18 time] overmuch anger, lying, * trickery, deception and swearing. For whoever fasts in any other manner falls short and sins, and it would 30 have been better if he had not fasted at all. As some of the Fathers have said, « The one who does not fast at all is better than the one

---

[33] *1 Tm. 2, 8.*

[34] I.e. Prime, Tierce, Sext, Nones, Vespers, Compline and Lauds.

[35] I.e. the Lord's Prayer.

[36] The reference here is to *Tafsīr al-Anājīl al-Muqaddasah*, which appears in the list of Ibn al-Muqaffa''s works given by Abū 'l-Barakāt ibn Kabar. See GRAF, *Zwei Dogmatische Florilegien der Kopten*, p. 62. The work is however now lost.

who merely abstains from bread and water», since [such a person] has not complied with the conditions we have mentioned.

Our fasting should last for nine hours of the day. Then we should begin our prayer, glorification, praise and recitation from the liturgical 5 portions of the books of God.

The evening, and a little time before, is to be set aside for our leisure.

That which has been slaughtered and that which has been hunted is excluded from our diet during this fast; the eating of all such things 10 is forbidden to us during the days of fasting — may God benefit us in abstaining from [such food].

Our predecessors have transmitted this to us, having received it from their predecessors, and so on back to the first generation, each succeeding age maintaining, on the authority of its predecessor, 15 that it had followed the example of those who had gone before them, and had abstained from [such food]. The fact that [such food] is not allowed to us when we are fasting is shown by [the practice of] ancient times, since the prophets and others who fasted did not eat anything except the plants of the earth; among them were Daniel, Ezekiel, 20 Ezra and others.

We must also, over and above these forty days, fast two days in every week, Wednesday and Friday; this is essential.

The remaining days during which we are to fast are the fasts of the apostles, the fast at Advent, the fast of the Virgin and the fast 25 of Nineveh [37]. These are customary usages which were established by many leading figures; hence whoever does not adhere to them is obtuse, in error and thoughtless.

XI. OUR STATEMENT ON REST DAYS

God has allowed us to do good works on all days — Saturday, 30 Sunday, and the rest of the days, and has forbidden us to do evil on any day.

We do not say that * He has forbidden us to give alms and do good * p. 19 on Saturday, as the Jews maintain; almsgiving and charity on feast days are among praiseworthy, good actions.

---

[37] I.e. the fast of Jonah, commemorating the fast of the Ninevites at the preaching of the Prophet Jonah, observed on the Monday, Tuesday and Wednesday of the week preceding Septuagesima Sunday.

We should honour Sunday especially by going to church, praying and standing in the presence of God with great joy in the great favour He bestowed on us on this day, because He saved mankind from the wickedness of Satan the Accursed, and demonstrated for us the truth of the Resurrection and Rising [from the dead] by his Resurrection. 5

We must make Christmas Day a day of rest, and also the Day of Sacrifice, that is, Epiphany, the Day of the Ascending, that is, the Feast of the Ascension, and Whitsunday, which is the day on which the Paraclete descended.

All this is in accordance with the terms we have mentioned regarding 10 the doing of good and the shunning of evil.

Honouring days [devoted to] the memory of the martyrs is obligatory, as the apostles commanded.

XII. Our Statement Regarding Almsgiving

As regards almsgiving, each one of us must give alms as he is able 15 according to his means. If he is poor he will be rewarded for this according to his ability, not according to the gift, as the Gospel prescribes [38] in reference to the woman who offered the two mites, and he should never come across a poor man without being charitable towards him and giving him [something] and doing his utmost [for 20 him], as the apostles commanded.

We must visit the captives, visit the sick, protect strangers, cover the naked, feed the hungry and give the thirsty to drink. These are duties obligatory upon us which the Gospel commands us to do [39].

Everything that we have said applies to believers and unbelievers 25 equally, but our care for the believers, whom the Gospel has described, and who are brethren who have made us love them the more, [should be] better and greater.

The proof, in the matter of the unbelievers, is the saying of the
* p. 20 Bible that : * « If your enemy is hungry, feed him, and if he is thirsty, 30 give him to drink, for by so doing you will be heaping coals of fire upon his head » [40].

---

[38] Mk. 12, 42.
[39] Cf. Mt. 25, 35-36.
[40] Ro. 12, 20.

XIII. Our Statement on Food

God, Whose name is blessed, has forbidden us to eat carrion, blood
and that which has been torn by wild beasts, as the Book of Acts [41]
states, and sacrifices to idols, as the apostle says, and similar things.
5 It is for every nation and people to follow their own customs in
regard to their food, according to the nature of their countries,
except for what we have said concerning carrion, blood and what has
been torn by wild beasts, for this is forbidden, and to eat it is not
allowable for any of the believers, Arab, non-Arab, Greek, Byzantine,
10 Ethiopian, Dailamite, Persian or Turk.

That which has been specifically forbidden or allowed by the Torah
has been abrogated by the law of Christ. That is simply for a parti-
cular reason which we have already explained with other matters in
our books against the Jews, and since our purpose here is to be concise
15 we have not brought forward a large number of considerations [for
discussion], the only point of which is to serve as arguments against
it [43], because you only asked us to describe our doctrines, not to
adduce arguments against our opponents.

XIV. Our Statement on Specific Penalties and Judgments

20 In regard to specific penalties and judgments we shall merely
give a simplified account with general comments.

The question of highway robbers, thieves, murderers, and those who
terrorize the highway, or the like, * is one in which the people of each   * p. 21
town and each ruler in every area should proceed in accordance with
25 their [own] laws, the customs of their countries and the usages inherited
from their forbears. However, as regards those whom the apostles
have described as « accepting » a fault, it is necessary for them to make
restitution equivalent to their fault at specified times. Sanctions
against wrongdoers and sinners vary, and the punishments differ;
30 priests among them are to be unfrocked if they commit mortal sins.

It is these of whom the apostle was speaking when he said : « No
one shall enter the Kingdom if they commit them » [44]. Their punish-

---

[41] Cf. *Ac.* 15, *20.*
[42] Cf. *1 Co.* 8, *1.*
[43] I.e. the Torah.
[44] Cf. *1 Co.* 6, *9.*

ment is to be expelled from the community and banished from the church, and the believers shall cut off [all ties of] friendship with them, and shall refrain from talking to them and mingling and mixing with them.

Whatever is taken by way of theft from the Houses of God shall 5 be returned together with five times its value, if there is one thief.

XV. Our Statement on Marriage

Our marriage rules vary because [certain] conditions are laid down for priests by the Bible. They are : do not marry a widow or a divorcee or a whore. The priest may not marry someone else after his first 10 wife['s death]; this is the consensus among Christians, except for the heresy introduced by Timothy the Catholicos [45], in permitting the Nestorians to marry after [the death of] the first wife, as they wish, one after another, even though the [number] might reach seven.

Similarly Abraham the Patriarch, lord of his people, [permitted] 15 a priest [to marry] as I have described, and also a bishop, presbyter and deacon.

However, they also differ from us on another matter, [since according to us] a deacon may marry after taking orders, but a bishop or a presbyter may not marry after taking bishop's and priest's orders. 20 This does not apply to the two sects which we have mentioned : * p. 22 I mean [those of] Timothy *the Catholicos and Abraham the Patriarch, for they allow [marriage] to the presbyter and the deacon, as I have previously said.

Later on our predecessors accepted other views regarding [the 25 marriage of] bishops; the Egyptians hold the view that the Bishop in Alexandria especially should be celibate [46] and not marry while in his sacerdotal state.

The Nestorians and the Syrians hold the view that the bishop should never be one of those who have married before taking episcopal 30 orders. The Nubians act in accordance with the discipline of the early church.

---

[45] I.e. Timothy I. He died in A.D. 823 in his 95th. year. For his life and works see W. WRIGHT, *A Short History of Syriac Literature* (London, 1894), pp. 191-194; A. BAUM-STARK, *Geschichte der Syrischen Literatur* (Bonn, 1922), pp. 217-218; I. ORTIZ DE URBINA, *Patrologia Syriaca* (2nd edition; Rome, 1965), pp. 215-216.

[46] This appears to be the meaning required for this illegible word.

The reason why a bishop should not have a wife is that he should have become a monk before taking episcopal orders.

The Nubians were not obliged to take monastic vows before taking episcopal orders, unless they chose to do so. This usage is also current 5 in the country of the Nestorians.

Everything I have said about bishops has a [good] reason [for it] and a correct procedure [to be followed in regard to it], but this is not the place to deal with them.

As for the laity, they are allowed to marry a virgin or maiden. 10 If his first wife has died [a man] may marry a second time, but if he refrains it is better. As regards a third, or further wives, the person who contracts such marriages commits an offence; in our opinion he has sinned greatly and has given no thought [to the matter].

In our opinion marriage is only allowable to our brethren of full 15 age, not being parties to disputes regarding property or contracts.

It is not allowable for a Christian to have carnal relations with slaves; as for infidel [slaves], carnal relations with them are [also] forbidden.

As regards the People of the Religion [47], and those of them who 20 have been enslaved, we do not know how matters stand in their country; possibly women marry priests or other [ordained] persons; or perhaps [the clergy merely] draw up the marriage contracts of other women and bless their dowries.

It is not allowable for us to have relations with nuns, because that 25 is forbidden to us, and to our opponents.

* XVI. Our Statement on Divorce   * p. 23

Divorce is not allowable for us after a marriage has been contracted through prayer, supplication and blessing, and in the presence of the officiant, except on account of proved fornication only, that is, 30 adultery.

Timothy the Catholicos allowed his followers grounds for divorce other than those stated in the Gospel: incontinence, drunkenness, madness and leprosy.

If a wife commits adultery, she betrays her husband, and puts 35 asunder what God has joined; and their punishment by God shall be great. In such a case [a husband] must separate himself from her

---

[47] This vague phrase apparently refers to the Western (Roman Catholic) Church.

and be rid of her. It is not allowable for any of the believers to marry
her; indeed she remains a disgrace for ever and a dishonour to the
community, and people should refrain from mixing with her and
associating with her, for as the Gospel [48] says : « Whoever marries a
divorced person is a fornicator », and as the apostle says : « Do you [5]
not know that he who is joined with a harlot is one body with her ? »[49].

XVII. Our Statement on Slaves

Serving their masters cheerfully is an obligation upon slaves, and
they must hearken to them. Their masters do not have the right
to harm them, and they are not to impose on them more than they [10]
can bear, for if they injure them they sin, since we are all servants
of God, as the apostle says.

I would prefer that every believer should refrain from enslaving
those adversaries who belong to the people of the [various] Christian
communities, who are taken captive. If someone buys [a slave], he [15]
should offer to emancipate him and [let him] go [back] to his home
and his country, for he may have sons and daughters and infants who
* p. 24 need to be looked after, and who would be * grief-stricken by his loss.

It could be that a man's wife is made captive, who may have borne
him sons and daughters, with no one to look after them and serve [20]
them.

A priest or other clergyman is not allowed to give him in marriage [50], and a priest is not allowed or permitted to marry a slave,
nor be enslaved.

This is my view on slaves.   [25]

Thus concludes the book *The Lamp of the Intellect*. May God have
mercy on us through the prayers of ... (?)
Amen. Amen. Amen.

The humble, sinful copyist asks every person who peruses this
[work] to pray for the forgiveness of his sins. Whatever he shall say, [30]
he shall receive compensation for it.

48 *Mt. 5, 32.*
49 *1 Co. 6, 16.*
50 I.e. the man whose wife is in captivity.

INDEX OF BIBLICAL REFERENCES

References are to the pages of the Translation.